How to draw Animals

Leonie Pratt and Louie Stowell

Designed and illustrated by
Non Figg, Antonia Miller, Katie Lovell
and Jan McCafferty

Edited by Fiona Watt

Contents

Elegant giraffes

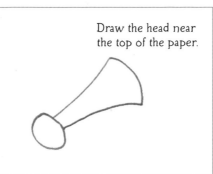

Draw the head near the top of the paper.

1. Using a pencil, draw an oval for a giraffe's nose. Draw two curved lines coming out from the nose, then add a curve for the top of the head.

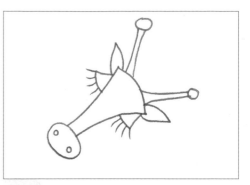

2. Draw the ears, then add triangles below them, for the eyes. Add eyelashes and nostrils, then draw horns on top of the giraffe's head.

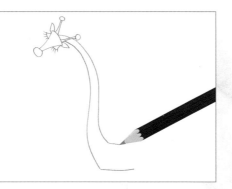

3. Draw one long curve and one slightly shorter curve for the giraffe's neck. Add a line for the tummy, then draw the rest of the body.

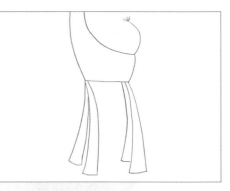

4. Add four long legs below the body. The legs should be narrow at the top and get a little wider at the bottom. Draw a tail, too.

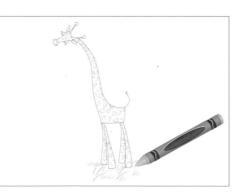

5. Use a pale orange wax crayon to draw circles all over the giraffe's body. Then, draw grass around the feet using a green wax crayon.

The wax crayon will resist the paint.

6. Fill in the giraffe and the grass with watery paints. Then, when the paint is dry, draw over the pencil lines with a thin black pen.

You could draw an insect flying around your giraffe.

If you want to do a
giraffe stretching up
to eat some leaves,
draw its head
upside down.

Bunny in a burrow

1. *Use a white pencil to draw a circle for a bunny's body on some brown paper. Draw an oval on top of the circle, for the head.*

2. Draw two long ears. Add shapes for the arms and legs. Draw a little circle for the tail on one side of the body. Then, fill in the bunny.

3. *Use a pencil to draw around the ears and head. Draw around the arm and along the back, then add little lines around the tail.*

4. Draw a curved shape for the front leg, like this. Draw a curve around the tummy, then draw outlines around the other leg and the arm.

For a large burrow like this one, draw all the bunnies and vegetables on a large piece of brown paper. Draw a wiggly burrow around them, then paint the soil.

You could paint sky at the top of your picture, then add grass and flowers.

5. Add dots for eyes and draw a small 'V' for the nose. Draw a curved mouth and whiskers. Then, draw little lines on the bunny's paws.

6. Fill in the nose with a pink pencil and add patches inside the ears and on the tummy. Then, draw a wavy shape for a burrow around the bunny.

7. Use brown paint to fill in the soil around the burrow. When the paint is dry, use pencils to draw worms and bugs in the soil.

You could use the ideas on this page to draw cats doing lots of different things.

Armchair cats

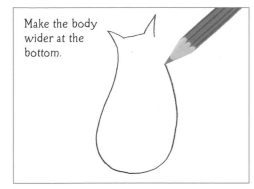

Make the body wider at the bottom.

1. Draw a short line for the top of a cat's head. Add two pointed ears on either side of the line, then draw a long curved shape for the body.

2. Draw a long tail curving out from the bottom of the body. *Use thick red paint to fill in the cat, then leave the paint to dry.*

3. *Use a black felt-tip pen to draw around the cat. Draw a line down the middle of the body, then add a line on either side of it, for the legs.*

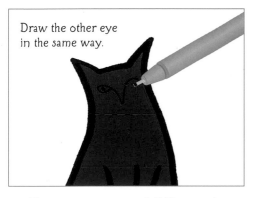

Draw the other eye in the same way.

4. Draw a curved 'V' on the head using a thin black pen. For the cat's eye, draw a curve under one end of the 'V' and add a dot inside.

5. Draw a triangle for the nose, then draw a curved mouth and long whiskers. Add stripes using a blue chalk pastel or a pencil.

Sleeping cat

Don't draw all the way around the head.

1. Draw the ears and the top of the head. Draw a small curve for the chin, then draw a large curved shape for the body.

2. Add a long tail and a shape for one of the front paws. Fill in the cat and let the paint dry. Then, go around the outline with a felt-tip pen.

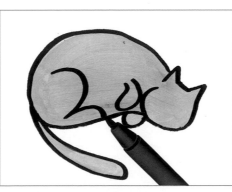

3. *Use the felt-tip pen to draw the other front paw next to the cat's head. Then, draw two curves for the back leg, like this.*

4. Add the face using a thin black pen, but draw the eyes closed. *Use a chalk pastel or a pencil to draw a zigzag along the cat's back.*

Playful penguins

You could draw an iceberg and some sea, then fill them in using watery paints. When the background is dry, glue your penguins onto it.

For a swimming penguin, draw curves on the feet, and glue the beak onto the top of the head.

The fish were drawn on shiny paper, then cut out and glued on.

1. *Use a blue pencil to draw a wide arch for a penguin's body on some black paper. Add the bottom of the body, with a tail on one side.*

2. Draw an arch for the tummy and add flippers on either side of the body. Then, cut around the penguin, leaving a small border.

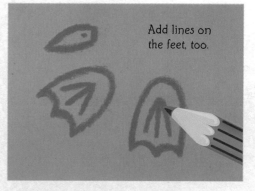

Add lines on the feet, too.

3. *Use a dark orange pencil to draw a beak on a piece of orange paper. Then, draw two feet with curves along the bottom, like this.*

This iceberg was filled in with watery blue paint. Then, thick white paint was brushed roughly over the top when the paint was dry.

4. Cut out the beak and the feet. Glue the beak onto the penguin. Then, glue the feet onto the back of the body, at the bottom.

5. Fill in the tummy using a white pencil. Draw small white circles for the eyes, then add dots inside with a black pencil.

Watery elephants

1. Draw a big oval for an elephant's body. Add a circle for the head on one side of the body. Then, draw four thick legs.

2. Draw two curves for the elephant's trunk, then draw a small 'U' between the ends. Add a pointed tusk beside the trunk.

3. Add an ear and draw some water coming out of the trunk. Then, erase the lines at the top of each leg and inside the ear and head.

Use pink, yellow and orange paint for a sunset sky like this one.

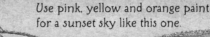

The elephants were drawn before the watering hole and horizon. Then, everything was filled in with watery paints.

Draw a line on the tusk, too.

4. Brush around the outline of the elephant using watery yellow paint. Then, while the paint is wet, blob some pale orange paint on top.

5. Clean your brush, then mix some pale purple paint. Fill in the elephant, but don't paint the end of the tusk, or the water. Let the paint dry.

6. Draw over the pencil lines with a purple pencil. Add an eye and a tail, then draw the toenails and little lines along the top of the trunk.

Sneaky sharks

1. Draw a long curve for the top of a shark's body on a piece of blue paper. Then, add two curves for a smiling mouth, like this.

2. Draw a curving line for the bottom of the body. Then, draw two triangles at the end of the body for the tail fin.

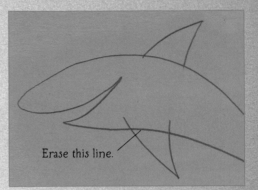

Erase this line.

3. Add a fin on top of the body, then draw a longer fin on the side of the body. Erase the pencil line where the fin overlaps the body.

4. Draw over the pencil lines using a thin black pen. Then, add an eye and a nostril, and sharp teeth inside the mouth. Add gills on the body, too.

5. Mix some watery blue paint and brush it inside the shark's outline. Then, paint the sea around the shark with thicker dark blue paint.

To draw a scene like this one, draw lots of sharks on a large piece of blue paper. Paint the sharks and the sea, then add the chalk details when everything is dry.

6. When the paint is dry, use white chalk or a chalk pastel to fill in the middle of the body and fins. Smudge the chalk a little with your finger.

These little fish were drawn with chalk, then some were outlined using a black pen.

Counting sheep

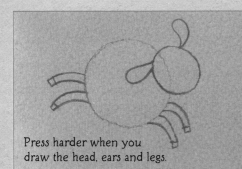

Press harder when you draw the head, ears and legs.

1. Pressing lightly with a purple pencil, draw a circle for a sheep's body on pink paper. Draw the head, then add the ears and legs.

2. Draw lots of big spirals all over the sheep's body, to look like wool. Then, draw a spiral at the back of the body, for the tail.

3. Use a darker pencil to draw a small 'V' for the nose and add a curling mouth. Draw circles for the eyes, then add dots inside.

4. Use white chalk or a chalk pastel to fill in the body and tail. Then, smudge the chalk around a little, to make the edges blurred.

5. Fill in the head, ears and legs using a purple chalk, then smudge it a little. Add white inside the eyes and pink dots for the cheeks.

6. Use yellow chalk to draw a line along the tummy and a smaller line under the tail. Smudge the yellow lines a little, too.

The hill, moon and stars were drawn after the sheep, then filled in with chalk.

Shaggy dogs

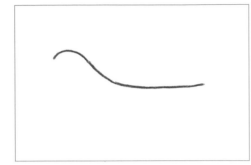

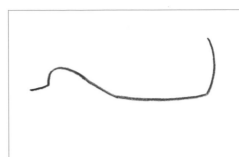

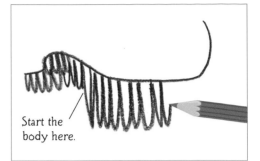

Start the body here.

1. *Use a brown pencil to draw a small curve for the top of a dog's head. Then, draw a long line for the neck and back.*

2. Draw the front of the head and a short line for the muzzle. Then, add a curved tail joining onto the back of the body.

3. Starting at the end of the muzzle, scribble lots of little lines for the dog's head and neck. Then, scribble longer lines for the body.

4. Scribble along the tail, then add legs and ears. Draw a black nose, then use a bright pencil to add a line for the collar.

For a sitting dog, draw a slanted line for the back.

Press hard with your pencil to draw a floppy ear.

For a dog like this, draw a long coat with no legs.

16

Draw sloping eyebrows to make a lion look really angry.

Grumpy lions

1. Mix yellow paint with a little red to make orange. Paint a circle for a lion's head. Add a neck, then paint an oval for the body.

2. Paint thick lines for the legs and add blobs for paws. Then, add a blob for the end of the tail a little way from the body. Let the paint dry.

3. Draw a line for the tail with an orange pencil. Then, use two different shades of orange to scribble a mane around the lion's head.

4. Use a thin black pen to draw a long nose and a mouth. Draw ears and eyes, and add whiskers. Then, draw lines on the paws and tail.

For a lioness, leave out the mane in step 3.

Big bear and baby bear

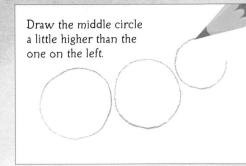

Draw the middle circle a little higher than the one on the left.

Erase the lines inside the outline.

1. Draw two circles next to each other, about the same size. Add a slightly smaller circle near one side, for the baby bear's head.

2. Draw curved lines to join the two larger circles. Then, draw more lines for the neck. Add shapes for the snout and the ear.

3. Add a leg under each of the larger circles. Then, draw around the outline of the bear using a blue pencil. Erase the other pencil lines.

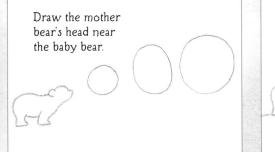

Draw the mother bear's head near the baby bear.

Draw a line for the ground, too.

4. Draw a circle for the mother bear's head. Then, draw a big slanted oval for the shoulder and a big circle for the back of the body.

5. Add curves for the neck and body, then add a snout and an ear. Draw the blue outline, then erase the other pencil lines.

The mother bear has long wavy lines drawn on her body, to make her look very furry.

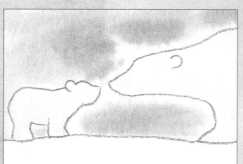

6. *Use a clean paintbrush to brush water around the bears. While the paper is wet, blob pale blue paint onto the background, for the sky.*

7. *Clean the paintbrush, then brush very pale yellow paint just inside the outline of each bear. Leave the paint to dry.*

8. *Use a pencil to draw the bears' faces. Then, draw small blue lines along the outlines, for fur. Add more fur on the bodies using a yellow pencil.*

Crafty crocodiles

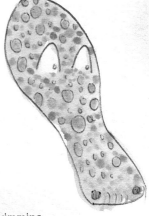

1. *Use a pencil to draw a long curving line for one side of a crocodile's body. Then, start at the top of the first line, and draw another line next to it.*

2. Draw two small arches for the crocodile's eyes. Add a long nose, then draw a wavy line for the mouth. Draw the chin, too.

For a swimming crocodile, draw three shapes for the head, body and tail. The rest of the crocodile is hidden under the water.

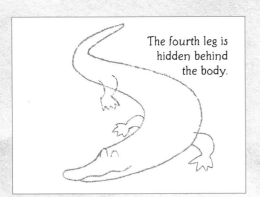

The fourth leg is hidden behind the body.

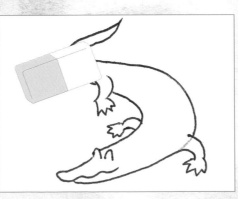

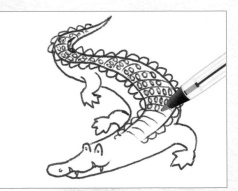

3. Draw two thick legs with pointed toes on either side of the crocodile, near the head. Add another leg, near the tail.

4. *Use a ballpoint pen to draw around the legs. Then, draw around the rest of the crocodile's outline. Erase the pencil lines inside the legs.*

5. Add some teeth, a nostril and dots in the eyes. Draw two lines curving along the crocodile's back, then add lots of scales all over the body.

You could use the ideas on these pages for different patterns of scales.

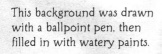
This background was drawn with a ballpoint pen, then filled in with watery paints.

6. *Use different shades of green felt-tip pens to fill in the scales. Add lots of dots and lines in the spaces between the scales, too.*

7. Dip a paintbrush into some clean water, then brush it over the crocodile. The green inks will bleed together, and fill in the crocodile.

Roaring tiger

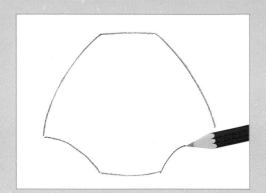

1. Draw a line for the top of the tiger's head. Add two curves for the side of the head. Then, draw a shape for the jaw, like this.

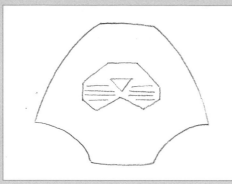

2. Draw a muzzle in the middle of the tiger's face. Add a triangle for a nose, then draw whiskers on either side of it.

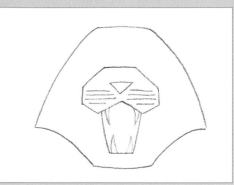

3. Add a long shape below the muzzle, for the tiger's open mouth. Then, draw curved, pointed teeth at the top and bottom.

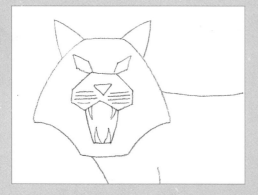

4. Draw two diamonds at the top of the muzzle for the eyes, then add curved triangles for ears. Draw lines for the back and leg, too.

Leave white shapes in the ears.

5. Use a black pencil to draw thick outlines over all the pencil lines. Draw curved shapes and dots in the eyes, then fill in half of each ear.

6. Draw a row of little triangles along the curves of the jaw and fill them in. Then, draw stripes around the eyes, like this.

7. Add more stripes on the face, around the muzzle. Then, draw long curved stripes along the back and on the leg.

8. Shade in the tiger with an orange pencil, leaving some white patches on the face and body. Fill in the mouth and nose with pink pencils.

Make the lines on the face spread out from the nose.

9. Draw over the shading with lots of dark orange lines to give texture to the fur. Don't draw lines over the white patches.

You could use green pencils to draw tall grass behind the tiger.

Curious meerkats

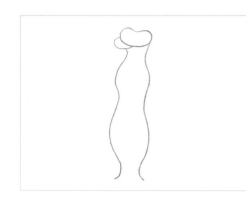

Add little claws on all the meerkat's paws.

1. Draw a bean shape for the meerkat's head. Add a shape for the nose. Then, draw curving lines for the body and legs, like this.

2. Draw the back legs and the tail. Then, add the front legs curving into the middle of the body. Draw a mound and grass behind the meerkat.

3. Erase the pencil lines inside the head. Draw ovals for the eyes and add dots inside. Then, add the nose, mouth and ear.

Paint the nose, too.

4. Brush pale orange watery paint along the top of the head, the sides of the body and the tail. Paint the mound and grass with yellow paint.

5. Mix some brown watery paint. Brush paint down the front of the body and on the front paws. Then, paint the ear and around the eyes.

This baby meerkat was drawn using the same shapes as the adult meerkat.

To make a scene like this, draw several meerkats standing in little groups, then add the mounds and grass and fill everything in.

For the back view of a meerkat, draw the head, then add ears on either side and draw a bump for an arm. Then, fill in the meerkat, leaving no white patches.

Sea horses

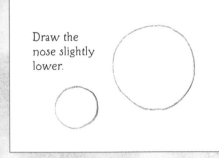

Draw the nose slightly lower.

1. Draw a circle for the side of a horse's head. Then, draw a smaller circle a little way away from the first one, for the nose.

2. Add a line from the top of the large circle to the top of the small one. Then, draw a curve to join the bottom of the circles.

3. Draw pointed ears at the top of the head. For the eye, draw two small curves. Add a line for the top lip, then draw the nostril and neck.

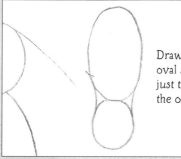

Draw the small oval so that it just touches the one above.

Leave space for the mane between the ears.

4. For a horse facing the front, draw a long oval with a smaller oval below it. Then, add two small curves to join the shapes.

5. Draw the ears, eyes and nostrils, then add a shape for the mouth. Draw curves for the body coming down from either side of the head.

6. Use a blue ballpoint pen to draw around the horses. Add wavy lines for the manes, and curls for waves. Erase all the pencil lines.

Dip a dry brush in thick white paint and run your finger over the bristles to flick 'sea spray' onto your picture.

Add some lines on the horses, too.

7. Use a white wax crayon to add swirls and bubbles in the waves. The crayon lines are shown in yellow here, so that you can see them.

For a horse like this, draw legs and hooves like these before you add the waves.

8. Brush watery blue paint over the paper. Then, while the paint is wet, add darker blue paint between the horses and on the waves.

Big city mice

The curves for the eyes should meet in the middle.

1. Draw a curved line for the bottom of a mouse's body. Add a shape for the rest of the body and head that curves in then out, like this.

2. Draw big round ears on top of the head and add shapes inside. Then, draw the feet at the bottom of the body. Add lines for the toes.

3. For the eyes, draw a big curve below each ear. Draw lines for the eyelids, then add a small circle inside each eye.

This apple core was drawn first, then the mouse was drawn around it.

28

You could draw tall buildings like these in the background.

Leave the eyes and tummy white.

4. Draw a curve with a little oval in the middle, for the nose. Add lines for whiskers and shapes for the paws. Then, draw a wavy tail.

5. Fill in the mouse's ears, body and tail with blue watery paint. *Use* pink paint to fill in the eyelids and feet, then leave the paint to dry.

6. *Use* a black felt-tip pen to draw over the pencil lines. Then, fill in the circles in the eyes, leaving a small white dot inside each one.

Draw two mice with their tails overlapping. Erase lines where the tails cross, then fill in the mice.

Mischievous monkeys

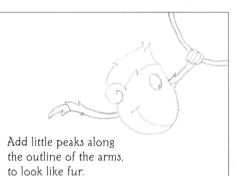

Add little peaks along the outline of the arms, to look like fur.

1. Draw a curve for a monkey's forehead. Add a nose, chin and a spiral for an ear. Draw fur on the head, then add an eye and mouth.

2. Draw two wavy lines for an arm, then add a pointed shape for a hand. Draw the other arm with thin ovals for fingers. Then, add a creeper.

3. Add a round tummy and draw fur around it. Then, draw curved legs and add the feet. Draw a long tail that curls at the end.

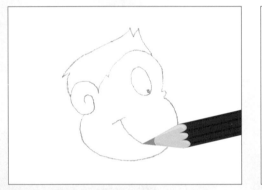

Fill in the creeper, too.

4. Fill in the monkey using different shades of brown paint. Let the paint dry, then draw over the pencil lines with a brown felt-tip pen.

For a surprised monkey, draw an oval mouth.

You could add 'whoosh' marks to show that the monkey is swinging.

The monkeys and the background were drawn first, then filled in with paint and outlined using felt-tip pens.

Sitting monkey

1. Draw two arches for the forehead, then add spirals on either side for ears. Draw a big chin, then draw the eyes, nose, mouth and fur.

2. Draw the tummy and add fur around it. Draw the arms with ovals for the fingers. Add the legs and tail, then draw the creeper, like this.

3. Use watery paints to fill in the monkey and the creeper. When the paint is dry, use felt-tip pens to draw over all the pencil lines.

Sleepy fox

Smudge blue chalk or chalk pastel along the top of the grass for the sky.

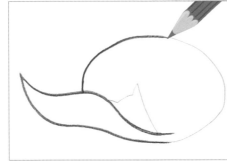

1. *Use a pencil to draw a bushy tail and a curved body. Add a pointed face with ears. Then, go over the lines with a brown pencil.*

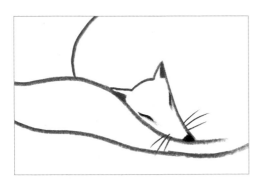

2. Draw brown patches inside the ears. *Use a black pencil to draw a triangle for the nose. Then, add lines for the eyes and whiskers.*

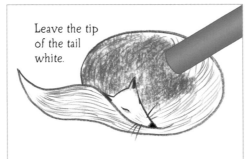

Leave the tip of the tail white.

3. Draw lines for fur on the tail and body with orange and brown pencils. Then, fill in the fox with orange chalk or a chalk pastel.

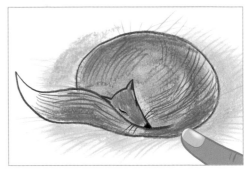

4. Smudge the chalk with your finger. Draw grass around the fox using green pencils, then smudge green chalk on top.

Digital manipulation by John Russell
First published in 2006 by Usborne Publishing Ltd., 83-85 Saffron Hill, London, EC1N 8RT, England www.usborne.com